DINOSAUR FACT DIG

CARNOTAURUS

AND OTHER ODD MEAT-EATERS

THE NEED-TO-KNOW FACTS

BY
JANET RIEHECKY

Consultant: Mathew J. Wedel, PhD
Associate Professor
Western University of Health Services

CAPSTONE PRESS
a capstone imprint

A+ Books are published by Capstone Press,
1710 Roe Crest Drive, North Mankato, Minnesota 56003
www.mycapstone.com

Library of Congress Cataloging-in-Publication Data
Names: Riehecky, Janet, 1953- author.
Title: Carnotaurus and other odd meat-eaters: the need-to-know facts / by Janet Riehecky.
Description: North Mankato, Minnesota: Capstone Press, [2017] | Series: A+ books.
Dinosaur fact dig | Audience: Ages 6-8. | Audience: K to grade 3. | Includes bibliographical
references and index.
Identifiers: LCCN 2015046628| ISBN 9781515726951 (library binding) | ISBN
9781515726999 (pbk.) | ISBN 9781515727033 (ebook (pdf))
Subjects: LCSH: Dinosaurs--Juvenile literature. | Carnivorous animals--Juvenile literature.
Classification: LCC QE861.5 .R54 2017 | DDC 567.91--dc23
LC record available at http://lccn.loc.gov/2015046628

EDITORIAL CREDITS:
Michelle Hasselius, editor; Kazuko Collins, designer; Wanda Winch, media researcher;
Gene Bentdahl, production specialist

IMAGE CREDITS: All images by Jon Hughes except: MapArt (maps), Shutterstock: Elena
Elisseeva, green gingko leaf, Jiang Hongyan, yellow gingko leaf, Taigi, paper background

Printed in China.
022016   002586

**NOTE TO PARENTS, TEACHERS,
AND LIBRARIANS:**
This Dinosaur Fact Dig book uses
full-color images and a nonfiction
format to introduce the concept of odd
meat-eating dinosaurs. Carnotaurus and
Other Odd Meat-Eaters is designed to
be read aloud to a pre-reader or to be
read independently by an early reader.
Images help listeners and early readers
understand the text and concepts discussed.
The book encourages further learning by
including the following sections: Table of
Contents, Glossary, Critical Thinking Using
the Common Core, Read More, Internet
Sites, and Index. Early readers may need
assistance using these features.

TABLE OF CONTENTS

CARNOTAURUS. 4

COELOPHYSIS 6

DAHALOKELY 8

DEINOCHEIRUS. 10

DELTADROMEUS. 12

EORAPTOR 14

HERRERASAURUS 16

INCISIVOSAURUS. 18

LILIENSTERNUS 20

MASIAKASAURUS. 22

RUGOPS 24

SHUVUUIA. 26

YAVERLANDIA 28

GLOSSARY. 30

CRITICAL THINKING USING THE
COMMON CORE 31

READ MORE 31

INTERNET SITES 31

INDEX 32

Carnotaurus and other odd meat-eaters were hunters that had sharp teeth, keen eyesight, and good senses of smell. They walked on two legs. Their arms were much shorter than their legs. They walked or ran with their stiff tails straight out behind them to keep their balance.

Some dinosaurs were very large, such as Carnotaurus. Others were small, such as Shuvuuia. Read on to learn more about Carnotaurus and other odd meat-eaters.

CARNOTAURUS

PRONOUNCED: KAR-no-TOR-us

NAME MEANING: meat-eating bull

TIME PERIOD LIVED: Late Cretaceous Period

LENGTH: 26 feet (8 meters)

WEIGHT: 1 to 4 tons
(0.9 to 3.6 metric tons)

TYPE OF EATER: carnivore

PHYSICAL FEATURES: two horns on
its head; sharp teeth; big claws

CARNOTAURUS' horns were
5.75 inches (15 centimeters) long.

CARNOTAURUS' arms
were even shorter than
Tyrannosaurus rex's arms.

Carnotaurus lived in what is now Argentina.

N
W E
S

where this dinosaur lived

The fossilized skin of **CARNOTAURUS** left marks on rocks around it. This showed the dinosaur had scales all over its body.

COELOPHYSIS

PRONOUNCED: SEE-lo-FY-sis

NAME MEANING: hollow form

TIME PERIOD LIVED: Late Triassic Period

LENGTH: 9 feet (2.7 m)

WEIGHT: 20 to 50 pounds (9 to 23 kilograms)

TYPE OF EATER: carnivore

PHYSICAL FEATURES: sharp teeth; long claws; long legs

Thousands of **COELOPHYSIS** fossils have been found at Ghost Ranch, New Mexico. Scientists think these dinosaurs died in a flash flood.

Coelophysis lived in what are now New Mexico and Arizona.

where this
dinosaur
lived

COELOPHYSIS is the state fossil of New Mexico.

Two types of **COELOPHYSIS** fossils have been found. One has thick bones. The other has thin bones. Scientists think the dinosaurs with thick bones were males. The dinosaurs with thin bones were females.

DAHALOKELY

PRONOUNCED: dah-HA-loo-KAY-lee

NAME MEANING: small thief

TIME PERIOD LIVED: Late Cretaceous Period

LENGTH: 9 to 14 feet (2.7 to 4.3 m)

WEIGHT: 441 pounds (200 kg)

TYPE OF EATER: carnivore

PHYSICAL FEATURES: strong legs; long tail; large head

Most scientists use Latin or Greek words to name dinosaurs. But paleontologist Andrew Farke used a language from Madagascar to name **DAHALOKELY**.

Dahalokely lived on flat plains in what is now Madagascar.

When **DAHALOKELY** lived, the islands of Madagascar and India were connected.

where this dinosaur lived

The only **DAHALOKELY** bones found so far are parts of its ribs and backbone.

DEINOCHEIRUS

PRONOUNCED: dy-no-KY-rus

NAME MEANING: terrible hand

TIME PERIOD LIVED: Late Cretaceous Period

LENGTH: 36 feet (11 m)

WEIGHT: 6.5 tons (6 metric tons)

TYPE OF EATER: omnivore

PHYSICAL FEATURES: long arms and legs; sail on its back

Scientists discovered **DEINOCHEIRUS'** arms and claws in 1965. The dinosaur's body wasn't discovered until 2009.

Deinocheirus lived in the forested area of what is now Mongolia.

N
W E
S

where this
dinosaur lived

DEINOCHEIRUS belonged to a group of ostrichlike dinosaurs. It was the largest member.

DEINOCHEIRUS swallowed stones to help it grind up tough plants. Scientists found 1,400 of these stones near the dinosaur's fossils.

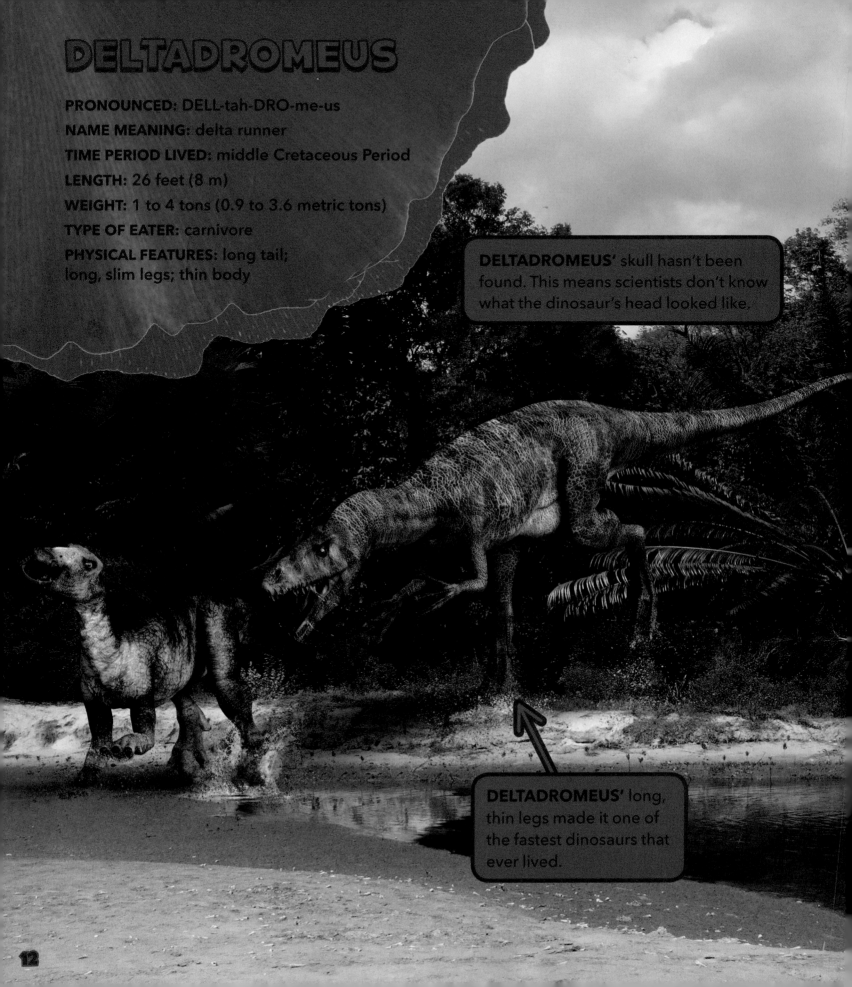

DELTADROMEUS

PRONOUNCED: DELL-tah-DRO-me-us

NAME MEANING: delta runner

TIME PERIOD LIVED: middle Cretaceous Period

LENGTH: 26 feet (8 m)

WEIGHT: 1 to 4 tons (0.9 to 3.6 metric tons)

TYPE OF EATER: carnivore

PHYSICAL FEATURES: long tail; long, slim legs; thin body

DELTADROMEUS' skull hasn't been found. This means scientists don't know what the dinosaur's head looked like.

DELTADROMEUS' long, thin legs made it one of the fastest dinosaurs that ever lived.

Deltadromeus lived in what is now Morocco.

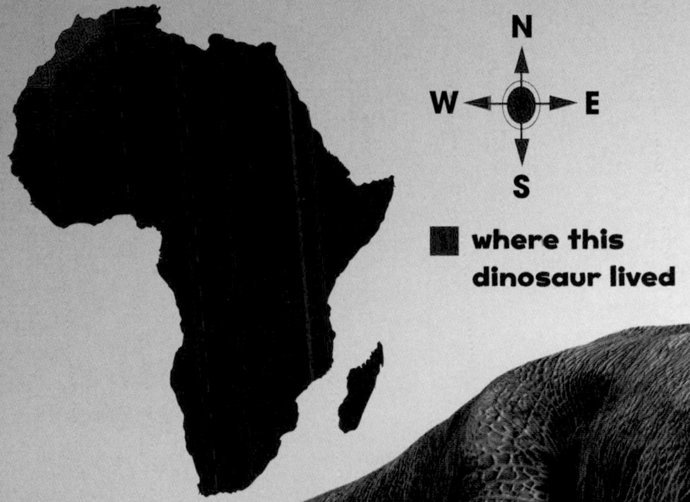

N
W — E
S

■ where this
dinosaur lived

DELTADROMEUS lived in the same area as two huge carnivores, Carcharodontosaurus and Spinosaurus.

EORAPTOR

PRONOUNCED: EE-oh-RAP-tur

NAME MEANING: dawn thief

TIME PERIOD LIVED: Late Triassic Period

LENGTH: 3 feet (0.9 m)

WEIGHT: 20 to 50 pounds (9 to 23 kg)

TYPE OF EATER: omnivore

PHYSICAL FEATURES: long legs; hollow bones; small head

EORAPTOR had two kinds of teeth. It had sharp teeth for cutting. Flatter teeth helped it grind or chew.

Scientists think **EORAPTOR** was one of the earliest dinosaurs on Earth.

Eraptor lived on a floodplain in what is now Argentina.

N
W · E
S

where this dinosaur lived

Only a few other types of dinosaurs lived at the same time as **EORAPTOR**.

HERRERASAURUS

PRONOUNCED: huh-RARE-uh-SAWR-us

NAME MEANING: Herrera's lizard; named after the man who discovered its fossils, Oswald Reig Victorino Herrera

TIME PERIOD LIVED: Late Triassic Period

LENGTH: 13 feet (4 m)

WEIGHT: 500 to 1,000 pounds (227 to 454 kg)

TYPE OF EATER: carnivore

PHYSICAL FEATURES: strong legs; short arms; sharp claws

Only 6 percent of the fossils found near **HERRERASAURUS** are from dinosaurs. Many other creatures lived in the area.

Herrerasaurus lived on a floodplain in what is now Argentina.

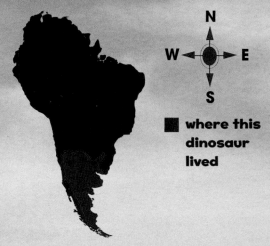

N
W ← → E
S

■ where this dinosaur lived

HERRERASAURUS was big. But it wasn't as big as the huge crocodile-like reptile Saurosuchus. Saurosuchus likely hunted Herrerasaurus.

HERRERASAURUS was one of the first meat-eating dinosaurs to walk on Earth.

INCISIVOSAURUS

PRONOUNCED: in-SIZE-ee-voh-SAWR-us

NAME MEANING: incisor lizard; named for its long incisor teeth in the front of its mouth

TIME PERIOD LIVED: Early Cretaceous Period

LENGTH: 3 feet (0.9 m)

WEIGHT: 1 to 5 pounds (0.5 to 2.3 kg)

TYPE OF EATER: herbivore

PHYSICAL FEATURES: long legs; feathered body; long front teeth

INCISIVOSAURUS is a member of a dinosaur group called Oviraptorids.

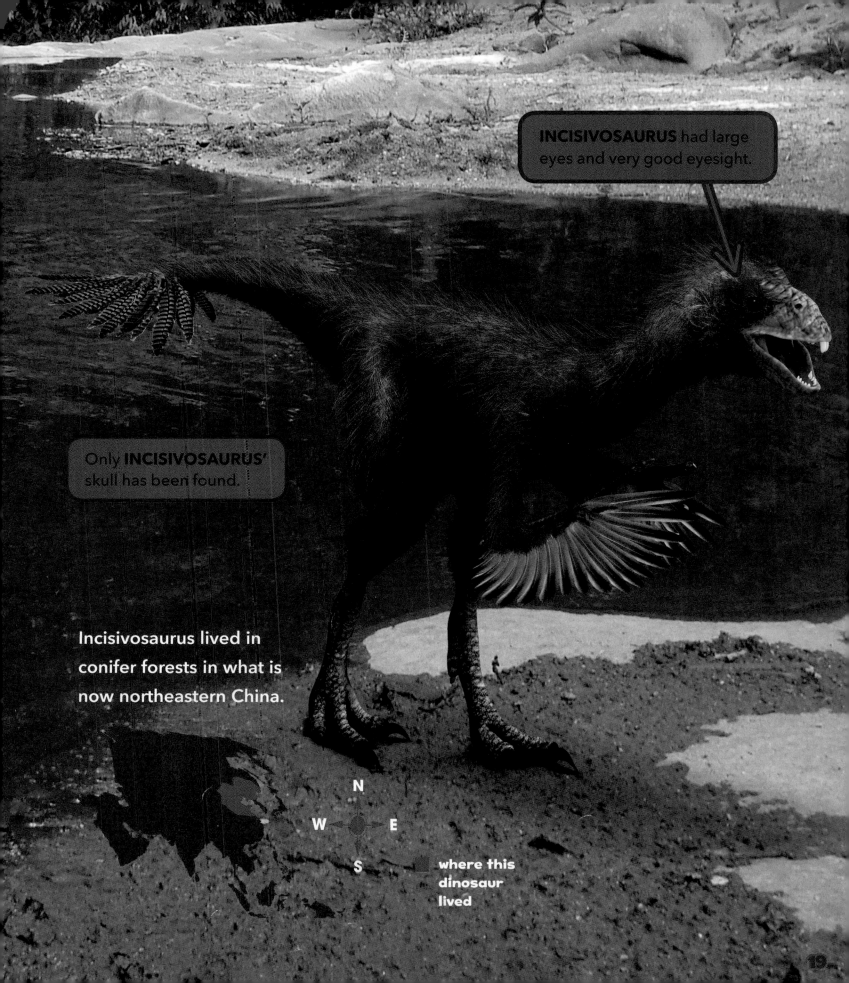

INCISIVOSAURUS had large eyes and very good eyesight.

Only **INCISIVOSAURUS'** skull has been found.

Incisivosaurus lived in conifer forests in what is now northeastern China.

N
W E
S

where this dinosaur lived

LILIENSTERNUS

PRONOUNCED: LIL-ee-en-STIR-nus

NAME MEANING: Lilienstern's lizard; named after amateur German paleontologist, Dr. Hugo Ruhle von Lilienstern

TIME PERIOD LIVED: Late Triassic Period

LENGTH: 17 feet (5.2 m)

WEIGHT: 200 to 500 pounds (91 to 227 kg)

TYPE OF EATER: carnivore

PHYSICAL FEATURES: short arms; long legs and tail; sharp claws

LILIENSTERNUS was the largest known predator of its time.

LILIENSTERNUS was a good hunter. It also may have been a scavenger.

Liliensternus lived near rivers and lakes in what is now Germany.

N
W ← → E
S

■ where this dinosaur lived

Scientists only have a few pieces of **LILIENSTERNUS'** skull. Scientists think the dinosaur had a crest on its head like Dilophosaurus because their bodies were so similar.

MASIAKASAURUS

PRONOUNCED: MAS-ee-ah-ka-SAWR-us

NAME MEANING: vicious lizard

TIME PERIOD LIVED: Late Cretaceous Period

LENGTH: 4.5 to 7.5 feet (1.4 to 2.3 m)

WEIGHT: 20 to 50 pounds (9 to 23 kg)

TYPE OF EATER: carnivore

PHYSICAL FEATURES: long legs and tail

MASIAKASAURUS is the only known carnivore that had teeth that bent forward.

Masiakasaurus lived in what is now Madagascar.

N
W ↔ E
S

☐ where this dinosaur lived

MASIAKASAURUS was fully grown at about 8 to 10 years old.

The scientists who found **MASIAKASAURUS** listened to music from the rock band Dire Straits. They decided to name the dinosaur Masiakasaurus knopfleri in honor of the band's lead singer, Mark Knopfler.

RUGOPS

PRONOUNCED: ROO-gops

NAME MEANING: wrinkle face

TIME PERIOD LIVED: Late Cretaceous Period

LENGTH: 19.7 feet (6 m)

WEIGHT: 1 to 4 tons (0.9 to 3.6 metric tons)

TYPE OF EATER: carnivore

PHYSICAL FEATURES: strong legs; small, thin teeth; long tail

RUGOPS' skull is wrinkled. Most skull bones are smooth.

Rugops lived in what is now Niger in Africa.

where this dinosaur lived

Only **RUGOPS'** skull has been found so far.

RUGOPS has two rows of holes on its snout. The holes may have held a crest. It could have used this crest to attract a mate.

SHUVUUIA

PRONOUNCED: SHOO-vu-YOU-ia

NAME MEANING: Mongolian word for "bird"

TIME PERIOD LIVED: Late Cretaceous Period

LENGTH: 2 feet (0.6 m)

WEIGHT: 1 to 5 pounds (0.5 to 2.3 kg)

TYPE OF EATER: omnivore

PHYSICAL FEATURES: feathered body; strong arms; long legs

SHUVUUIA lived during the same time as other small carnivores, such as Velociraptor, Saurornithoides, and Gobivenator.

Shuvuuia lived in what is now Mongolia.

N
W E
S

where this
dinosaur lived

SHUVUUIA is the first
birdlike dinosaur found
with a complete skull.

SHUVUUIA had short, strong arms for digging, like
a mole. It also had long, light legs for running, like a
roadrunner. No creature alive today is quite like it.

YAVERLANDIA

PRONOUNCED: YAV-ur-LAN-dee-uh

NAME MEANING: named after Yaverland, where its fossils were found

TIME PERIOD LIVED: Early Cretaceous Period

LENGTH: 8 feet (2.4 m)

WEIGHT: 110 pounds (50 kg)

TYPE OF EATER: omnivore

PHYSICAL FEATURES: large eyes; long feathers on arms

YAVERLANDIA probably used sight instead of smell to find food and stay away from danger. The part of its brain used for smell was small.

Only one **YAVERLANDIA** fossil has been found so far. It is from the top of the dinosaur's skull.

Yaverlandia lived in what is now the Isle of Wight in England.

YAVERLANDIA belongs to the group of dinosaurs that are the closest relatives to birds.

N

W   E

S

where this dinosaur lived

GLOSSARY

BACKBONE (BAK-bohn)—a set of connected bones that run down the middle of the back; the backbone is also called the spine

CARNIVORE (KAR-nuh-vor)—an animal that eats only meat

CONIFER (KON-uh-fur)—a tree with cones and narrow leaves called needles

CREST (KREST)—a flat plate of bone

CRETACEOUS PERIOD (krah-TAY-shus PIHR-ee-uhd)—the third period of the Mesozoic Era; the Cretaceous Period was from 145 to 65 million years ago

FLASH FLOOD (FLASH FLUHD)—a flood that happens with little or no warning, often during periods of heavy rain

FOSSIL (FOSS-uhl)—the remains of an animal or plant from millions of years ago that have turned to rock

HERBIVORE (HUR-buh-vor)—an animal that eats only plants

HOLLOW (HOL-oh)—empty on the inside

OMNIVORE (OM-nuh-vor)—an animal that eats both plants and animals

PALEONTOLOGIST (pale-ee-uhn-TOL-uh-jist)—a scientist who studies fossils

PLAIN (PLANE)—a large, flat area of land with few trees

PREDATOR (PRED-uh-tur)—an animal that hunts other animals for food

PRONOUNCE (proh-NOUNSS)—to say a word in a certain way

SCALE (SKALE)—a small piece of hard skin

SCAVENGER (SKAV-uhn-jer)—an animal that eats animals that are already dead

SNOUT (SNOUT)—the long front part of an animal's head; the snout includes the nose, mouth, and jaws

TRIASSIC PERIOD (TRYE-az-ik PIHR-ee-uhd)—the earliest period of the Mesozoic Era; when dinosaurs first appeared

CRITICAL THINKING USING THE COMMON CORE

1. Why do scientists think Carnotaurus had scales all over its body? (Key Ideas and Details)

2. Liliensternus was a hunter and scavenger. What is a scavenger? (Craft and Structure)

3. How is Rugops' skull different from most dinosaur skulls? (Key Ideas and Details)

READ MORE

Gregory, Josh. *Coelophysis*. Dinosaurs. Ann Arbor, Mich.: Cherry Lake Publishing, 2016.

Hughes, Catherine D. *First Big Book of Dinosaurs*. National Geographic Little Kids. Washington, D.C.: National Geographic, 2011.

Riehecky, Janet. *Show Me Dinosaurs: My First Picture Encyclopedia*. My First Picture Encyclopedias. North Mankato, Minn.: Capstone Press, 2013.

INTERNET SITES

FactHound offers a safe, fun way to find Internet sites related to this book. All of the sites on FactHound have been researched by our staff.

Here's all you do:

Visit *www.facthound.com*

Type in this code: 9781515726951

Super-cool stuff! Check out projects, games and lots more at **www.capstonekids.com**

INDEX

arms, 4, 10, 16, 20, 26, 27, 28

claws, 4, 6, 10, 16, 20

crests, 21, 25

discoveries, 6, 7, 9, 10, 11, 16, 19, 25, 29

Early Cretaceous Period, 18, 28

eyes, 19, 28

Farke, Andrew, 8

horns, 4

Late Cretaceous Period, 4, 8, 10, 22, 24, 26

Late Triassic Period, 6, 14, 16, 20

legs, 6, 8, 10, 12, 14, 16, 18, 20, 22, 24, 26, 27

middle Cretaceous Period, 12

range, 5, 7, 9, 11, 13, 15, 17, 19, 21, 23, 25, 27, 29

sails, 10

skin, 5

skulls, 12, 19, 21, 24, 25, 27, 29

teeth, 4, 6, 14, 18, 22, 24